Scrum

Step-by-Step Agile Guide to Scrum

(Scrum Roles, Scrum Artifacts, Sprint Cycle, User Stories, Scrum Planning)

Jason Bennett & Jennifer Bowen

Table of Contents

Introduction

Introducing Scrum

Scrum is a straightforward, easy-to-use collaborative framework in which teams work together to effectively, optimally and creatively deliver desired outcomes and products. Scrum is an amazing system that allows you to break down large and complex problems into small, achievable tasks, which can be delegated to individual team members.

As a beginner, you notice that experienced techies use the terms scrum and agile interchangeably. However, the two are different and understanding the difference is, perhaps, the best way to begin understanding scrum.

Agile is a collection of practices and methods set up in the Agile Manifesto that includes elements such as cross-functionality of teams, self-organization, collaboration and more.

Scrum, on the other hand, is the actual framework that employed for the implementation of the Agile-based development.

Think of it as a diet and a recipe. Suppose you are following a vegetarian diet that has a set of principles and methods to follow to achieve a particular health-related goal.

Now, the recipe of chickpea taco is a framework, which you use to implement the vegetarian diet. Agile is like the diet, and Scrum is like the recipe.

Agile was developed from various project management techniques used by Japanese organizations in the '70s and '80s. Jeff Sutherland together with Ken Schwaber created the Scrum framework based on Agile techniques to facilitate, initially, the timely and smooth delivery of software products and projects.

Benefits of Using Scrum

There are multiple benefits of using Scrum to implement Agile techniques in any project or product development. Here are some of those benefits:

Low time-to-market – Scrum facilitates the introduction of new features incrementally through Sprints. At the end of each sprint, a releasable product with the new increment is available.

Therefore, Scrum allows you to monitor, release and meet deadlines and other requirements at each stage of the project instead of having to wait for the release at the end of the entire project.

Keeping track of each stage ensures the product releases earlier than scheduled.

Increased returns – As the product is released earlier than scheduled or on time, the returns on investment start coming in faster resulting in increased accumulation of revenue over time.

Moreover, as problems and issues are tackled at each stage by all concerned stakeholders, the product is bound to be completed satisfactorily in all respects thereby increasing its marketability. Therefore, the product released with Scrum has a high potential for increased returns.

Quality and Transparency – Scrum-processed products undergo testing at each sprint allowing for early detection and solving of problems and issues. All stakeholders and product owners are involved in all stages of the development process, which makes the entire exercise very transparent.

The incremental improvements and changes also give immense flexibility with lowered risk.

Scrum Glossary

Mastery of the glossary and other technical jargon of Scrum facilitate the understanding of this framework better. Some of the terms mentioned here are not necessarily Scrum glossary but are used commonly by users.

Burn-down chart – This chart reflects remaining efforts Vs. Time. Though not a compulsory requirement in all Scrum projects, the burn-down chart helps in improving transparency of progress.

Burn-up chart – This reflects the increased measure of the progress of work Vs. Time. Again, burn-up charts are an optional element. However, they facilitate increased transparency.

Daily Scrum – A daily timed event of 15 minutes or less, the daily Scrum allows the development team to plan the next day's work during a sprint after discussing the current day's work.

Definition of done – is a list of expectations that the developed software must live up to before it can be released into production. This element is understood, defined, and managed by the entire Scrum Team.

Development team – is part of the Scrum team and is responsible for organizing, managing, and doing all the developmental works and activities to create an incremental releasable product.

Emergence – This term explains the unforeseen emergence of a new and unexpected fact or piece of knowledge.

Empiricism – It is a kind of process control in which only what has happened in the past is taken as correct and for sure. All decisions are based on experimentation, observation, and experience.

The three irrefutable pillars of empiricism are adaptation, transparency and inspection.

Engineering standards – is a set of technology and development standards employed by the development team to create incremental releasable software.

Forecast – The selected items from the Product Backlog by the development team to include into a sprint is referred to as forecast (of functionality).

Increment – a small piece of working software that adds to the existing set of working increments and the sum of all the increments put together forms the product.

Product Backlog – Managed by the product owner(s), the product backlog is a list of the work that needs to be completed to create and maintain a product.

Product Backlog Refinement - It is an activity that forms part of any sprint. In this activity, the development team and the product owner add granularity and refine the product backlog.

Product Owner – This is that role in a Scrum team, which is responsible for optimizing the value of the product that is under development.

The product owner's role includes expressing and managing functional and business expectations for the product to the development team(s).

Ready – The development team and the product owner arrive at a shared understanding of the level of description of all the items in the product backlog.

This understanding is referred to as 'ready' status and is introduced at the time of sprint planning.

Scrum Board – This is a physical board used by the Scrum team to make information visible to the entire Scrum Team.

The information on the scrum board is used to manage the sprint backlog.

Scrum Master – This role is responsible for assisting, coaching, guiding, and teaching the Scrum team on the understanding and use of Scrum.

Scrum Team – consists of the scrum master, the development team, and the product owner.

Scrum Values – This is a set of principles and values that underpin the effective working of the Scrum framework. These values include focus, commitment, respect, openness, and courage.

Self-organization – This is a crucial management principle of the Scrum framework wherein teams organize and manage their work autonomously.

Of course, it is important to remember that self-organization should happen with reference to given goals and within set boundaries.

Sprint – This is a timed event of not more than 30 days. The sprint acts as a container for all Scrum activities and events related to that timed event. Sprints take place consecutively with no intermediate gaps.

Sprint Backlog – is a detailed sketch of the development work needed to complete a Sprint and realize its goal. The sprint backlog is managed and maintained by the development team.

Sprint Goal – represents the purpose of the sprint briefly. Many times, the sprint goal is a business problem that needs a solution. Functionality could be adjusted during the sprint to achieve the sprint goal.

Sprint Planning – This is another timed event that should be completed in less than 8 hours. In this event, the scrum team inspects the product backlog and picks out the most valuable work to be included in the next sprint. Then, the scrum team designs the picked-up work into a sprint backlog.

Sprint Review – A timed event of four hours or less, the sprint review is done to conclude the work done during the sprint.

The stakeholders and the Scrum Team inspect the increment resulting from the particular sprint, assess its impact on the progress of the overall product, and update the necessary details on the product backlog.

Sprint Retrospective – This is an event to inspect the previous sprint. It is a timed event of three hours or less. Any points for improvement noted during the inspection are added to the next sprint backlog.

Stakeholder – This person is outside of the Scrum Team but has a specific interest in or knowledge of the product that is required to complete the increment.

The stakeholder is represented by the product owner and actively engages with the scrum team during the sprint review.

Velocity – This is an important element used to measure the development team's rate and value of work.

The velocity is an indication of the amount of incremental work completed from the Product Backlog.

Chapter One: Scrum Roles

The Scrum Team has the following Scrum Roles:

- The Product Owner
- The Development Team
- Scrum Master

Scrum teams are cross-functional and self-organizing. Self-organizing means that the team members are at liberty to choose how best to accomplish the given work. They are not directed by anyone outside of the team.

Cross-functional means that the team members are sufficiently competent in all the required functions without having to depend on anyone outside the team to complete the work.

The model of scrum roles or a scrum team is designed to maximize productivity, creativity, and flexibility. Scrum teams designed like this have proven to be increasingly effective in accomplishing complex jobs.

The Scrum teams deliver projects and products incrementally and iteratively resulting in maximizing feedback options. When Scrum Teams deliver incrementally 'done' products, it is ensured that at any given stage, a potentially usable version of the product is always available.

The Product Owner

The responsibility of the product owner is to maximize the value of a product that is being developed by the development team.

The methodology of maximizing value varies across individuals, Scrum Teams and organizations. The Product Owner is solely responsible for Product Backlog management. Managing product backlog includes:

- Expressing items on the product backlog in a clear and concise manner
- Ensuring all the necessary items on the product backlog are ordered to achieve missions and goals optimally
- Optimizes the value of the work done by the development team
- Ensuring the product backlog is transparent and visible to one and all and also contains the next item that the Scrum Team will work on
- Ensuring that the development team understands the items in the product backlog to the required extent

While the actual work can be done either by the product owner or a delegated person from the development team, the important thing to note here is that the product owner is accountable for all the tasks mentioned above.

Moreover, the product owner is a single individual and not a group or committee. The requirements and desires of a group of stakeholders' committee might be represented in the product backlog by the product owner.

However, any change in items or change in the prioritization of items in the product backlog has to be routed through and approved by the product owner.

The entire organization must respect the product owner's decision for that role to be a success. The product owner's decisions and the outcomes of these decisions are visible in the product backlog.

The development team is bound by the requirements and conditions laid down in the product backlog that is maintained and managed by the product owner.

The Development Team

The development team comprises of a set of professionals who work together to deliver a releasable increment of the 'done' product at the end of every Sprint.

The members of the development team are the ones responsible for creating the increment. A 'done' increment is a prerequisite at the Sprint Review.

Organizations powered by Scrum structure their development teams in such a way that are self-organizing which means to say that they organize and manage their work on their own. This self-organizing structure synergizes the development team's effectiveness and efficiency resulting in an optimized product.

The characteristics of a Scrum development team are:

- It is self-organizing to the point that even the Scrum Master cannot give it any mandate on how to work the items on the product backlog into potentially releasable done increments.
- It is cross-functional which means the team members are all skilled in the various functions in such a way that there is no need to look for people outside of the team to complete the assigned task or product increment
- There are no titles given to the members of the development team irrespective of the kind of work anyone does
- Additionally, there are no sub-teams defined in the Scrum development team irrespective of the domains such as architecture,

testing, business analysis, business, etc. that are included in the product increment

- Individual team members of a Scrum development team could have specialized areas of focus and skills. However, the development team is wholly accountable for the product increment

The Size of a Development Team – The optimal size of a development team should be small enough for nimbleness and large enough to accomplish all the required tasks defined within a Sprint.

A development team that has less than three members reduces the amount of interaction and also provides for decreased productivity. Very small development teams could face skill constraint challenges during the Sprint resulting in a less-than-optimized product increment or even in the failure to deliver the increment.

On the other hand, having a very large team could use up a lot of resources on management and coordination. Large teams run the risk of generating unnecessary complexities, which could come in the way of an efficient product increment delivery and defeat the purpose of an organized empirical process.

Looking at this scenario, Scrum recommends a development team size ranging between 4 and 9 depending on the needs and requirements of the product increment.

The Scrum Master

The responsibility of the Scrum Master is to promote and support Scrum and Scrum users by teaching and coaching them on the Scrum theory, practices, tools, values, and rules and regulations. The Scrum Master serves as a servant-leader of the team.

He or she helps people who are outside the team to understand the importance or non-importance of their interactions with the Scrum team.

The Scrum Master can alter these interactions in such a way that the value of work delivered by the Scrum Team is optimized.

The scrum master and the product owner – The Scrum Master offers a multitude of services to the product owner including:

- Making sure everyone on the Scrum Team understands the scope, goal, and the product domain as well as possible
- Finding new and innovative techniques to manage the product backlog effectively
- Coaching the Scrum Team on the importance of and how to update the product backlog with clear and concise items
- Making sure the Scrum Team understands empirical-based product planning
- Coaching and helping the product owner to arrange the product backlog items in a way to maximize value
- Ensuring Scrum events take place as and when needed or requested

The scrum master and the development team – The scrum master helps the development team in the following ways:

- Coaching the team in the ways of cross-functionality and self-organization
- Facilitating the production of high-value products and product increments
- Identifying and eliminating obstacles deterring the progress of work
- Facilitating scrum events
- Coaching the team members in areas wherein scrum implementation is partially adopted or not fully understood

The scrum master and the organization – The scrum master helps the entire organization in the following ways:

- Coaching and leading the organization through its scrum adoption process
- Helping the employees and other stakeholders to understand and implement the working of Scrum in an empirical environment
- Facilitating the improved productivity of the scrum team
- All the scrum masters work together to help in increased effectiveness of scrum implementation across the entire organization

Chapter Two: Scrum Artifacts, Tools, Concepts, and Practices

In the Introduction chapter, some of the scrum artifacts were discussed in brief. Let us understand them in a bit more detail now.

The discussions in this chapter include a few essential Scrum components that are representations of the value and work of the product development. Scrum artifacts are designed to provide transparency in the entire cycle.

They also provide opportunities to inspect progress and make necessary adaptations. Scrum artifacts maximize transparency by ensuring that everyone has the same understanding of all the information.

The Product Backlog

In simple words, the Product Backlog is the list of all the items and things that need to be done in the product. The items listed in the product backlog could be technical-centric or user-centric. The product owner is accountable for maintaining this artifact.

Other stakeholders including the Scrum Master, the Development Team(s), Scrum Team and others can contribute to the Product Backlog to get an extensive and complete artifact.

In addition to the Product Backlog, the Scrum Team is free to maintain other artifacts such as user role summary, descriptions of workflows, storyboards, and user interface guidelines.

However, these additional artifacts cannot replace the Product Backlog but can only be a complementary artifact to facilitate increased detailing of the various elements in the product.

The Product Backlog is used in all Sprint Planning Meetings to discuss the top relevant items mentioned there. The Scrum Team chooses which of the items go into the next Sprint. The Product Backlog is more than a simple to-do list and here are some of the important discerning features:

Any entry made into the Product Backlog should necessarily add value to the client – Every item in the Product Backlog should add value to the client without which that any item is a waste.

The items that add value could be in descriptions of nonfunctional and functional customer requirements, the list of work that requires to be done to launch the product, taking remediating effects, etc

All entries are ordered and prioritized accordingly, and it is a living document – The ordering and prioritizing is a continuous process and changes are made as and when required.

Items are modified or deleted to be replaced with new and updated items. No requirement or item is a frozen state, and that is the reason the Product Backlog is referred to as a living document.

Sprint Backlog

The Sprint Backlog is a list of tasks and items that are identified by the Scrum Team to be completed in a sprint. The Scrum Team picks up the top and relevant items from the Product Backlog that is feasible to be completed in the next Sprint and these items go into the Sprint Backlog.

The Team selects the size and the items of a Sprint Backlog so that the members are committed to completing the picked-up tasks during the Sprint. In addition to the relevant items taken from the Product Backlog, the Sprint Backlog also contains a plan on how to deliver the product increment and realize the Sprint Goal.

The team members are expected to update the Sprint Backlog as and when new information is received and at least once each day. Most Scrum Teams update the Sprint Backlog during the Daily Scrum.

The Scrum Master in conjunction with the Scrum Team estimates the amount of remaining work and the next day's work is allocated and updated in the Sprint Backlog.

The detailing in the Sprint Backlog should be sufficient for the members to clearly understand where they stand at the end of each day during the Daily Scrum. The Spring Backlog is also a living document and is modified and updated right through the duration of the Sprint.

Increment

The Increment at any stage of the product development is the sum of all the items and tasks on the Product Backlog that are completed. The increment is also the value of all the done increments from the previous Sprints.

An increment should be in the 'done' status at the end of each sprint. The 'done' status means the incremental work completed should be usable and potentially releasable.

An increment represents a body of work that is ready for inspection. Incremental, inspected work supports the empirical concept of Scrum operations. An increment can also be seen as a step towards achieving the goal of the final product release.

An important element to define a done increment is that it should be usable irrespective of whether the product owner chooses to release the increment or not.

Burn Charts

There are two kinds of burn charts that are used in Scrum; Burn Down Charts and Burn-up Charts. The Scrum Burn Down chart represents a visual graphical measurement of the completed work at the end of the day as against the projected work.

This helps everyone in the Scrum Team understand whether the project is on track or not. The visual information from the burn down chart (the completed work line moves downward toward zero) helps the Scrum Team to make adjustments to meet expected deadlines.

The Scrum Burn-Up Chart also charts (in a graph form) the progress towards completion. The most basic form of Burn-up charts consists of two lines including the project scope line (or total work line) and the work completed line. When these two lines meet, the project is completed.

A burn-up chart is useful in showing the concerned stakeholders how the project is moving and how any incremental demands or requirements can affect the deadline.

Task Board

The task board is simply a physical board that contains the user stories of the current Sprint along with the associated tasks and components. Typically, these things are displayed using post-it notes or index cards.

Ideally, the task board is divided into columns with descriptions such as stories, not started, in progress, and done going from right to left. As the progress of each story happens, the item is moved to the relevant column.

The task board is a great collaborative tool and can be very useful for product owners and scrum masters to track progress. Moreover, the task board enhances transparency as everyone can see how things are moving.

Definition of Done

The concept of 'done' in Scrum is a shared understanding of all stakeholders regarding the completion of the product or increment. Every member of the Scrum Team must have the same understanding of what constitutes a 'done increment.'

This shared understanding of the 'definition of done' helps everyone assess the progress in the same way and ensures every member of the Scrum Team is aligned with the final goal of the product development.

This definition of done helps the Development Team pick up the most relevant items from the Product Backlog for the next Sprint. Every sprint delivers increments that are releasable and usable as per the same definition of done. Each done increment is added to the previously done increments so that the entire thing works together and represents the definition of done up to that point in the product development.

As Scrum Teams become more knowledgeable and mature, the definition of done expands to include stringent criteria to achieve increasingly higher product quality.

Chapter Three: The Sprint Cycle

The heart of Scrum is the Sprint. It is a timed event of not more than one month. During the Sprint, a potentially releasable and usable product increment is created.

Ideally, the duration of each sprint of a product development remains more or less consistent. As soon as one sprint gets over, the next one starts immediately. A Spring Cycle has many components including:

- Sprint Planning Meeting
- Daily Scrum
- Story Time
- Sprint Review

The following points have to be borne in mind during each Sprint:

- No changes should be made that could negatively impact the Sprint Goal
- Goals concerning quality are not to be decreased
- The scope can be renegotiated and clarified between the development team and the product as more learning happens with the progress in the development work

Every Sprint must have a goal that is expected to be achieved along with a flexible plan and design that act as a guideline for the Scrum Team right through the Sprint. The Sprint Goal must include the details of the resultant product increment.

The duration of each Sprint should not be more than one month. If the time horizon is too far away, then the definition of 'done' could change giving rise to complexities and increased risk.

One-month sprints allow for inspection of progress at least once a month, thereby limiting risks and ensuring that the development work is on the expected track.

Sprint Planning Meeting

The description of the work that needs to be accomplished during the Sprint is discussed during the Sprint Planning Meeting. The planning of each sprint is a collaborative effort of the entire Scrum Team. For a one-month Sprint, the Sprint Planning Meeting should not exceed eight hours.

The duration of the meeting can be accordingly reduced if the sprint is for less than one month. It is the Scrum Master who ensures that the planning duration and the Sprint duration are kept within the time-box limits.

The outcome of the Sprint Planning Meeting should provide answers to the following two questions:

- What can be the incremental product delivery in this Sprint?
- What work needs to be done to accomplish the incremental product?

What can be the incremental product delivery in this Sprint? – The Development Team works on this aspect and picks up the relevant items from the Product Backlog to be included in this Sprint. The relevant items from the Product Backlog are picked up after the product owner discusses the Sprint Goal and what needs to be achieved at the end of this sprint.

It is a collaborative effort from the entire Scrum Team to clearly understand the value of the work and the definition of done in the Sprint.

The following inputs are needed to ensure a feasible plan is designed as an outcome of the Sprint Planning Meeting:

- The Product Backlog
- The latest product increment
- The projected capacity and the past performance of the development team

Only the Development Team gets the final say on what items can be picked up from the Product Backlog for the Sprint. This core principle of Scrum ensures that the development team remains committed to the Sprint Goal. The entire Scrum Team devises the Sprint Goal, and it serves as a guideline for the development team on why the increment is being built.

What work needs to be done to accomplish the incremental product? – Once the Sprint Goal has been decided and the items from the Product Backlog selected, the Development Team now decides on what needs to be done and how to work to achieve the Sprint Goal.

The plan to achieve and the items selected for the Sprint go into the Sprint Backlog.

The Development Team begins by designing the work and the system that are needed to convert the Product Backlog items into a working increment. While work can vary in size and efforts, sufficient planning is done at the Sprint Planning Meeting to enable the Development Team to project what they can achieve during the Sprint.

By the end of the Sprint Planning Meeting, the development team would have been able to plan the initial days of the sprint into batches of one-day work. It is important to remember that the development team is self-organized and chooses how to approach the work autonomously.

The product owner helps in trading-off items from the Product Backlog depending on whether the team has too little or too much to do during the Sprint.

At the end of the Sprint Planning Meeting, the development team should be in a position to let the Scrum Master and the Product Owner know how it plans to accomplish the Sprint Goal successfully.

Daily Scrum

This event is held every day during the Sprint and is only 15-minutes long. During the daily scrum, the development team inspects the work done since the previous day's daily scrum and plans for the next day's work.

The daily scrum optimizes the chances of meeting Sprint Goals as the development team meets every day to discuss and deliberate on how best to self-organize.

It is entirely up to the development team to run and manage the daily scrum. While some teams choose to answer preset questions, others choose the discussion format. No matter which format is used, the basic tenet of a daily scrum is to track progress towards the sprint goal.

The daily scrum is a necessary tool to be followed. However, after the daily scrum, the development team along with the other members of the Scrum Team could have detailed discussions based on the outcome of the daily scrum.

The daily scrum is the prerogative of the development team facilitated, if needed, by the Scrum Master.

During the 15-minute daily scrum, of other members of the scrum team are present, then it is up to the Scrum Master to ensure that these members do not disrupt the meeting. Daily Scrums are very useful for:

- Improving communications
- Eliminating the need for other developing related meetings
- Identifying the obstacles on a daily basis thereby making it easier to find solutions immediately
- Highlighting and promoting quick decision-making
- Improving understanding of the work being done

Story Time

This is usually a weekly meeting scheduled at the same location and at the same time every week. The entire Scrum Team including the product owner and the Scrum Master is involved in Story Time, the sole purpose of which is to go through the backlogs to prepare for the future.

During story time, new stories and epics could be added; large stories could be split down into smaller sizes for better implementation, etc.

Sprint Review

The Sprint Review is conducted at the end of every Sprint. It facilitates inspection of the incremental work done during the Sprint and Product Backlog adaptation and updates based on which the next Sprint can be planned. The increment work done is presented to foster collaboration and elicit feedback.

Sprint Reviews are of 4-hour duration for one-month Sprints, and for shorter sprints, the sprint review duration is appropriately reduced. The

Scrum Master facilitates the Sprint Review and ensures all the people attending it understand its true purport. Elements of a Sprint Review are:

- The Scrum Team and other key stakeholders (invited by the product owner attend it
- The product owner explains the 'done' items and the to-be-done items in the product backlog
- The development team discusses what worked well during the sprint and what didn't work well and how they overcame the problems
- The development team demonstrates the 'done' incremental work, and it also answers questions about the work done
- All the attendees collaborate to work out the next level of strategy including reviewing timelines, discussing potential capabilities and the budget, and how the product might have changed after the increment of the previous Sprint has been added to it

The outcome of a Sprint Review includes a revised and updated product backlog, which clearly defines the items for the next Sprint.

Chapter Four: User Stories

In Scrum, development tasks are not merely technical-sounding to-do lists. User stories are employed to explain users' system requirements, functional and non-functional end-uses, and other expectations from the product that is being developed.

Scrum gives a lot of importance to user stories primarily because through this process, the development team focuses on the user and his or her needs rather than treating the product development merely as a technical process.

User stories shift the focus of the technical development team from creating software codes mindlessly to solving customer problems with their technical skills. User stories are accurate representations of user desires and needs.

The success of any product development depends on the understanding of user needs by the team. User stories are a great way to achieve this precise and unambiguous understanding of user needs by the developers.

Typically in Scrum, the Product Backlog is a collection of all user stories. Of course, the product owner does not merely dump the user stories into the Product Backlog artifact but orders and prioritizes them to help the development team pick up the most important user stories to be included in the next Sprint.

How to Structure a User Story

User stories include a persona, the desire or need of this persona, and the benefits for the persona from the final product. A typical Scrum user story is structured as follows: As a (*the user type*) I want (*the user's desires or needs*) so that (*the benefits for the user from the product*).

Here is an illustrative example of a user story of a bank customer who wishes to use the ATM for cash withdrawal. As a *bank customer*, I want *an ATM to withdraw cash* so that *I need not wait in long bank queues.*

Such a structure helps in arriving at a clear and unambiguous definition of 'done.' The persona's needs automatically become the definition of done in the Scrum project.

Acceptance Criteria for User Stories

Acceptance criteria defined for user stories help in the accurate and complete representation of the needs of the persona. These criteria ensure that the user story is complete and all requisite conditions for meeting user needs are taken into consideration.

Acceptance criteria specify the conditions under which the user story needs to be fulfilled which ensures that the development teams clearly understand user demands thereby preventing any miscommunication or misinterpretation of user stories. Acceptance Criteria are used:

To clearly define boundaries – Development teams define the boundaries or conditions under which a user story is expected to be completed

To achieve consensus with the client – Acceptance criteria help clients and the Scrum Team to achieve consensus on what is expected to be delivered from the project

For testing purposes – Acceptance criteria help in testing whether the product or product increment has achieved the intended end use or not. It helps in checking if the system is working as per the client requirements.

To estimate and plan accurately – Acceptance criteria help the Scrum team to plan accurately and divide the user story into smaller tasks (or Sprints) in an incremental way to achieve the final product with almost guaranteed success.

Epics and Themes

So, a user story is a user-centric description of what the user wants. An epic in a Scrum project is a large-sized user story. There are no standard sizes based on which a Scrum user story can be called an epic. It is highly relative, and the Scrum Team can choose to call any story that they believe is big as an epic.

Ideally, epics are broken down into small-sized user stories, a practical collection of which can fit into one Sprint.

A theme is nothing but a collection of user stories. All the user stories that talk about a particular topic (for example, monthly report printing) can be together collected into one theme. When teams can group many stories into one theme, it helps in managing user stories in a better way.

Benefits of User Stories

Many people who are new to Scrum might look at user stories as a wasted effort when any big project can just be converted into a to-do list and get to work. However, in Scrum, user stories give a vital user-context, and the associated tasks come with a sense of value that they bring to the entire project. Here are some key benefits of using user stories:

User stories maintain the focus of the Scrum Team on the user – A simple to-do list focuses on the task at hand whereas a collection of stories keeps the focus of the team on solving problems for the end user.

Stories promote collaboration – When the user's end goal is clearly defined, then the team can collaborate and work together and find ways and means to achieve the defined user goals in the best possible way.

Stories promote creative thinking – Team members are encouraged to think critically and analytically to come out with solutions that help in achieving the desired end goal.

Stories drive momentum – As each story gets converted into tangible goals, the team members feel motivated and are driven to solve more challenging problems ensuring the final product is delivered smoothly and on time.

The acceptance criteria of user stories enhance clarity for the Scrum Team – As all user stories have to comply with the acceptance criteria, the Scrum Team is not left in any doubt about what the user wants from the product.

Writing User Stories

The following elements will have to be borne in mind while writing user stories:

Definition of done can be drawn out from the story - Only when the story's outlined task is clear, can you draw out an unambiguous definition of done which helps the Scrum Team achieve the desired goal.

User Stories should include tasks and subtasks – All the steps needed to complete the user story have to be clearly outlined and responsibilities for timely and correct completion need to be allocated to team members.

User Stories must have personas – Personas represent the people or the end-users of the product. User stories must include these personas.

If there are more than one kind of end-users, it might be prudent to have multiple user stories for the same product development work.

Ordered step – Every step in the larger process of the development work must have a corresponding user story.

Feedback from end-users – Instead of estimating the needs by yourself, it is a much better idea to speak to the end-users and take their feedback on what they want.

Be careful about time – Most Scrum Team forget to include this vital aspect of writing user stories. Stories have to fit into one sprint and therefore, long stories which could take months to complete must necessarily be broken down into multiple user stories which can be accommodated into sprints.

When the user stories are ready, then they need to be available for the entire Scrum Team and the other stakeholders to view.

Managing User Stories

A user story can be written by the user or the product owner and is submitted for review. Once the story is accepted, then it needs to be incorporated into the development workflow through the product backlog. At sprint planning meetings, the Scrum team decides which stories are to be tackled in the upcoming sprint.

At this stage, the team discusses the functionality and technical requirement of each user story. All these requirements are input into the story.

Another important aspect of managing user stories is to score each story into different types based on complexities involved or the time taken to be completed.

Scrum Teams use different methods of scoring user stories including T-shirt sizes, poker series, the Fibonacci sequence, etc. to arrive at accurate estimations.

Chapter Five: Scrum Planning Principles (The Product Roadmap)

A common misconception among early Scrum learners is they believe that planning is not an essential aspect of Scrum development. This idea could come from one of the core principles of Scrum, which is based on the empirical methods of inspection and adaptation.

One of the basic tenets of Scrum is that it is not possible to get all the things right at the stage of planning itself. The team has to continuously inspect, make changes, and adapt to changing dynamics of any development program.

While the above statement is true, it is wrong to believe that there are no planning schedules in a Scrum project.

There is some amount of upfront planning that happens and a healthy balance of upfront planning and tackling challenges as and when they encountered during the inspection process is an ideal roadmap to follow in Scrum development projects. Here are some essential planning principles that help in creating a seamless product roadmap.

Helpful but Not Excessive Upfront Planning

Excessively detailed planning at the beginning of the Scrum project is not just a waste of time and effort but could end up seriously deterring the progress of the development work.

However, leaving out upfront planning altogether results in negligence and is not right at all. Therefore, upfront planning involves taking steps to schedule elements of the work in a helpful but not excessive manner.

Planning Options Have To Remain Option Right Up To the Last Minute

Keeping planning options open until the last possible minute gives the team flexibility and power to make crucial changes. This means that elements that work best when planned at the last minute should not be planned upfront. Early planning based on inadequate and half-baked information is not a prudent Scrum planning principle.

Scrum Planning Focuses More on Replans and Adaptations Rather Than On Conforming To a Rigidly Fixed Plan

The Scrum approach to planning is to be flexible with the structure and shape of the plan to enable making adaptations instead of conforming to one single unchangeable plan.

Conforming to a fixed plan prevents the team from adapting to changing dynamics that take place throughout the product development process, which is bound to result in a less-than-optimal outcome for the client. Adapting to changing needs is the way Scrum Teams plan.

Planning Inventory Has to be Managed Sensibly

Creating a large volume of invalidated and predictive planning inventory in the form of charts, graphs, and other Scrum artifacts can prove counterproductive in a Scrum product development. Critical and real information is learned as and when the development work progresses based on which plans can be updated for the next phase.

If the team gets straddled with large amounts of wasteful artifacts that are based on invalidated upfront planning, the members will be forced to rewind and rework the plans thereby increasing risks and delaying the entire project.

Excessive planning inventory based on invalidated data results in many wastages including:

1. Efforts that were used in the detailed upfront planning that are to be discarded now
2. Significant waste of time and effort in upgrading and updating the plan with new and relevant data
3. Wasted opportunities of having to use time and effort to do point no (2) instead of working on real-time developmental work which would have taken the team closer to the goal

Planning inventory has also got to be managed sensibly and dynamically based on real information instead of invalidated data.

Scrum Planning Is Always Based On Small and Frequent Incremental Releases

Scrum planning is based on small and frequent incremental releases versus a single, large release. Frequent, small releases offer faster feedback and facilitate increased return on investment.

Scrum Teams Plan on Learning Fast and Changing Directions As and When Needed

No amount of upfront planning and detailing can help overcome dynamic challenges that keep coming up during product development. It is important for Scrum Team members to include the following elements in their planning:

- Pick up learning fast
- Implement the learning quickly
- Make swift changes as and when needed

Scrum planning principles include the knowledge that the teams must be ready to identify and accept that the current plan is not working well and changes are needed to the planning process to move toward a viable product. Learning is a critical goal in any Scrum Planning processes.

Scrum Planning Works on Time-Boxing

Sprint, sprint planning meetings, and all other Scrum events are planned on a time-boxing basis. The concept of time-boxing is an excellent time management technique that facilitates work organization and scope management. The time-box drives team members to work at a reasonably sustained pace in order to accomplish the task taken up. There are multiple other benefits to the concept of time-boxing, and some of these benefits include:

Time-Box Sets Up a Work-In-Progress Limit – Work-in-progress or WIP is a planning inventory that reflects work having started but not finished. Time-boxing is a tool that helps in limiting WIP so that there is something tangible to show as completed.

During the sprint planning meeting, the members take up only those tasks that they believe can be completed within the time-boxed sprint.

Time-box Forces Prioritization – It is obvious that not all elements of the development work have the same priority at any given point in time. A timed planning schedule will drive team members to take up those tasks that are an absolute priority at that stage.

This prioritization helps in sharpening the focus of the team to ensure the best possible incremental release is created.

Time-box Planning Demonstrates Progress – When the team completes and validates work scheduled to be completed by a known and accepted date, then there is a demonstration of progress of work.

This demonstrable value of work reduces organizational risk as it moves away from ambiguous forms of progress such as reporting conformity to plans, etc.

Time-box based planning also facilitates the demonstration of progress of large user stories, which might need more than one time-boxed sprint to complete.

Completing a part of the large piece of work ensures the client understands that measurable and valuable work is getting done at every stage.

Time-box Planning Prevents Undue Waste of Resources to Achieve the Elusive Perfectionism – When work is given to be completed without a reasonable deadline in place, very often, the efforts to find perfectionism is wasted more than necessary, especially in situations where good enough works equally well.

Time-boxing forces members to finish up the work reasonably well without wasting endless time and energy on striving for the elusive perfection.

Time-box Planning Drives Closure – When teams know that something has to be completed within a known date and time, they are driven to achieve closure in a dedicated way. A hard deadline compels team members to do their best to complete the work in the best possible way within the fixed deadline.

The absence of time-box results in decreased urgency to complete set tasks by the members.

Time-box Planning Provides Improved Predictability – As Scrum events are planned in small, frequent batches, it is easy to deliver improved predictability in the short time horizon.

This ability to predict the work that can be completed results in better management of the entire product development program.

In summary, Scrum Planning Principles are based on flexibility and adaptability rather than on conformity to a fixed plan that leaves no room for changes and improvements.

Chapter Six: Release Planning

The primary purpose of release planning is to define the contents of the potentially releasable incremental product. Release planning calls for high-level planning that could include elements of multiple Sprints.

Release planning serves as a guideline reflecting the expectations about the features and product increments that are going to be released. The core objectives of release planning include the following:

- To resolve discrepancies between the product roadmap and the team's commitment to what they can deliver during the release
- To extend predictability and visibility of the product development work beyond the sprint based on which the concerned stakeholders can take important budgetary and other planning decisions
- To provide the Scrum teams an opportunity to understand the progress made toward product completion

Release Planning Process

The following steps help you understand how release planning is done:

- Take the entire product or project and break it down into major features
- Separate them into absolutely important features that have to be delivered (called primary features) and the additional features that would be a nice addition to the product (secondary features)
- Now, this feature mix (in the form of user stories) fill up the Product backlog
- Now, place these features against the time-boxed development events (sprints)
- Your draft release plan is ready.

Now, look at the releases and make sure sufficient resources are available to complete the work within the set dates. Check out what kinds of interdependencies exist and make changes accordingly to the release plan. The following elements are needed to create an effective release plan:

- An estimated and prioritized Product Backlog
- The estimated velocity of the Scrum Team – For an existing team, knowing its velocity will help you immensely in release planning. However, for new teams and for existing teams whose velocities are not readily available, it can be easily gauged by observing and tracking a couple of Sprints performed by the development team
- Scope of work, goal, and available resources

Release planning requires a systematic approach. First, create a draft release plan or a preliminary roadmap. Include dates and other important resources to the plan. Make sure the release plan is updated after every sprint.

Testers are an important set of people to include in the release planning schedule. They do the following activities:

- Decide which of the team members will perform the testing activities
- Write user stories along with acceptance criteria for use by the testers (if not already done)
- Create the correct testing environment
- Create the testing data that needs to be used by the testers for testing
- Specify the scope and goal of testing and what testing activities to be carried out
- Clarify doubts on those user stories where data is insufficient or unclear

- Determine the testing strategy for the entire release
- Identify and inform concerned stakeholders about testing risks that might be encountered
- Define the various test levels that will be performed during the testing process

It would be unwise to work on a release plan until the Scrum Team has a product backlog that is clearly ordered, estimated, and prioritized.

The Iron Triangle and Scrum

Release planning can be effective if you understand the concept of iron triangle and how Scrum projects can work with it. The term 'iron triangle' was first coined in 1969 and represents a waterfall method to product development. Any product development program can succeed when the three significant constraints including scope, time, and resources are successfully managed.

The iron triangle is so called because you cannot alter one constraint without affecting the others. Here are the three constraints in a bit of detail:

- Scope – is the work that needs to be done including functionalities and features that deliver a working and viable product
- Resources – include team members, budget, equipment, etc. needed to execute and deliver the product
- Time – is the deadline for product delivery

In the conventional iron triangle, the scope is fixed while time and resources are variable factors. For product development, this means that the team will have to collect and define product requirements or the list of work items needed to complete the project. The schedule and resources can be changed to fit the fixed scope.

The iron triangle gives the Scrum Team an idea of the various elements that can be traded off in such a way so as to facilitate early delivery, reduced risks, and improved return on investment. For example, suppose a Scrum team is halfway through a particular project, and they realize that it might not be possible to finish the development within the deadline.

Now, the only constraints they can work with are time (they can ask for an extension) and resources (they can get more people to work on the project) resulting in increased costs. This is the waterfall approach.

In Scrum-based software development projects, the fixed constraints are time and resources with variable scope. Teams are committed to fixed time schedules (such as sprints), and resources (in terms of development teams) are also more or less fixed. By keeping these two elements fixed and consistent, teams are driven toward efficient and effective collaborative working developed through trust and continuity which, in turn, results in the release of a well-made product by a committed team.

It must be noted here that as projects get bigger and larger teams and longer duration Sprints come into play, keeping the scope varied with fixed time and date may not be viable. Long-term and large Scrum projects require even more flexibility in the iron triangle approach.

The Scrum Team needs to work dynamically and arrive at the right iron triangle approach suitable for each stage or each product development work. There are no right and wrong approaches.

The key element is to find the right iron triangle approach suitable for that particular release.

Chapter Seven: The Characteristics that Define an Outstanding Development Team

Any Scrum Team's success is highly dependent on the quality of professionals who make up the Development Team. These professionals are assigned the task of delivering a potentially usable product or product increment at the end of each Sprint.

How does one describe an outstanding Development Team? The people are the ones who can take any team from an average to an outstanding level. Here are some features that will help you discern such amazing team members that can create a great development team:

Excellence Is Their Forte

People who follow excellence can take any development team from the ordinary to the extraordinary. A great Scrum development team invariably employs the methods of Extreme Programming (XP) to achieve excellence. XP is equipped with multiple tools that drive development team to design and build excellent products.

Spike Solutions and Team Swarming Are Commonly Practiced

Spike solutions are a great way to solve very challenging architectural and technical problems encountered during product development. Team Swarming is a method, which entails the entire team to focus all their combined energies and resources on only a couple of items at a time. In fact, if the concerned is a bit large, then the focus of the team is restricted to only that one item. The team swarming method helps in completing tasks quickly as all resources are channelized together instead of scattering energies is different directions.

Updating Product Backlogs is a Committed Effort

A committed development team does not need prodding to update the product backlog regularly for improved transparency for the entire Scrum Team. The team understands that a well-maintained product backlog is the backbone of a successful Scrum project. Moreover, a dedicated team will always ensure that any element it picks up to do will be left in a better condition than it was when it was picked up.

A Cohesive Development Team Shares its Learning and Experiences

Sharing experiences is one of the most effective ways of learning. A good development team knows and appreciates this, and they are always on the lookout for new learning and new experience either through various meetings within the organization or attending external seminars.

A Good Development Team Knows It Can Never Be Endlessly Productive and Needs Some Slack

No human being can work productively without some break. A good development team understands that breaks for relaxing are important to keep productivity and creativity at high levels. Moreover, emergencies that keep need to be handled without slackness are a recurring theme in product development. So, a bit of slack during an average day is important to counter the pressures of emergencies.

Development Teams Treat Daily Scrums as Conversations

The term 'meeting' renders a needless sense of formality to the Daily Scrum and takes away the interesting aspects of the exchange. A cohesive development team treats daily scrums as interesting conversations in which the day's achievements, and challenges are discussed and preparations are made for the next day's work.

They Totally Understand Customers' Needs

A team that is in touch with its customers is a team that can understand their needs without any doubt. They truly know what the customer wants from the product development.

They Can Convert Technical Jargon to Business Value

A knowledgeable development team knows and appreciates the fact that technical jargon does not find favor with their customers and the non-technical members of the Scrum Team. Therefore, they can translate technical jargon into business value that can be understood by all stakeholders.

They Trust Each Other

It is impossible for any team to achieve success together if there is lack of trust. The members of an excellent development team trust each other implicitly knowing that the entire team is working toward the same goal.

They Deliver Features with Unerring Regularity

The members of a well-knit development team understand the value of resources that are being spent towards the development program. This knowledge drives them to work with determination so that new features are delivered at the end of each Sprint with unerring regularity.

A Good Development Team is Truly Cross-Functional

The skills of all the members of a great development team put together make the team self-sufficient in itself negating any need to look for outside help to accomplish the tasks. The members do not refer to themselves as playing any one particular role. Instead, they work cohesively to achieve the desired 'done' increment or product.

They Update the Scrum Board without Fail

A well-organized development team does not need to be told that the Scrum Board needs to be updated so that the Scrum Team knows where exactly the project is going. While a Scrum Master might facilitate the process, a good development team doesn't need any prodding from the Scrum Master to do this beneficial task.

They Spend Time and Efforts on Innovation

A good technical team understands the importance of innovation to stay relevant and create products that meet and exceed customer expectations. The members of such a team do not hesitate to spend time and efforts to innovate in order to keep up with the highly dynamic technology industry. Innovation is a necessity in today's competitive world, and a good development understands this very well.

They Don't Really Need a Definition of 'Done'

A great development team coupled with a deep understanding of their customer needs and their excellent technical skills really doesn't need a definition of 'done' to know when they have achieved their customer's desire. The reason for the definition of done is to keep the entire Scrum operation transparent.

They Know the Importance of Giving Objective Feedback to Each Other

A corollary to the 'trust' aspect of a good development team, this point is pertinent to ensure that all members respect each other. They learn the art of giving honest and upfront feedback and deeply appreciate the importance of 'impact' feedback, which is done immediately after the event. Feedback that is postponed for a later time could be ineffective and reactive. Hit the rod when the iron is hot but with respect and dignity.

A Champion Development Team Manages Its Team Composition Autonomously

Instead of waiting for help, a good development team manages to speak and collaborate with other teams to see if skilled people can be exchanged or moved depending on the needs of each team. They don't wait for skills to get into their team. Instead, they reach out and pull in specifically skilled people as and when needed.

A Supreme Development Team Practices Collective Ownership

Understanding collective ownership of the entire product development is a crucial element for its success. Therefore, members are rotated across the various development teams so that skills are shared and learned by everyone in the team. This rotation activity also encourages collective ownership.

They Handle Interdependencies on Their Own

The members of an outstanding development team manage interdependencies with other teams on their own. This attitude ensures there are no bottlenecks and roadblocks created on the path to achieving the desired Sprint Goal.

So, you can see that any good development team needs to have trust and respect for its members and their skills. They need to self-organize without any outside interference for which collection ownership of the problem at hand is a key element. The entire team should work as a single unit instead of coming across as an entity with squabbling members.

Conclusion

Scrum was designed to help in facilitating the obstacle-ridden path of software development. Any system intends to make the process smoother and easier to understand than before. Every element of Scrum is designed to meet this purpose.

While initially Scrum was founded for software development work, today it is used in multiple scenarios including but not limited to:

- Find viable product capabilities, markets and technologies
- Development technologies and products
- Release products and product enhancements, sometimes as often as thrice a day
- Develop and sustain cloud and other operational environments
- Maintain old products and create renewal products

The Scrum events, roles, and rules and specifics combine so that the development work is bound by a single framework resulting in the cohesiveness of the process and, in turn, a fabulous product that meets every expectation of the client.

Finally, no matter how good a system is designed, the effectiveness of its operation is highly dependent on the people using it.

Therefore, it is essential that you truly understand and appreciate the working of Scrum and then dive in to partake of its many benefits.

Resources

https://www.scrum.org/resources/what-is-scrum
https://www.scrum.org/scrum-glossary
http://www.dummies.com/careers/project-management/10-key-benefits-of-scrum/
https://www.thescrummaster.co.uk/scrum/benefits-scrum-agile/
http://scrumguides.org/scrum-guide.html
https://www.scrum-institute.org/The_Scrum_Product_Backlog.php
https://www.mountaingoatsoftware.com/agile/scrum/scrum-tools/sprint-backlog
http://www.clariostechnology.com/productivity/blog/whatisaburnupchart
https://manifesto.co.uk/agile-concepts-scrum-task-board
http://scrumguides.org/scrum-guide.html
http://blogs.collab.net/agile/story-time-the-hidden-scrum-meeting
https://www.atlassian.com/agile/project-management/user-stories
https://rubygarage.org/blog/clear-acceptance-criteria-and-why-its-important   https://www.mountaingoatsoftware.com/blog/stories-epics-and-themes
http://www.innolution.com/essential-scrum/table-of-contents/chapter-14-scrum-planning-principles
http://www.innolution.com/blog/the-benefits-of-timeboxing
https://www.quickscrum.com/Help/185/sg-Release-Planning,
https://www.atlassian.com/agile/agile-at-scale/agile-iron-triangle
https://www.scrum.org/resources/what-is-a-scrum-development-team
https://www.scrum.org/resources/blog/25-characteristics-great-development-team